W9-BNV-905

# RHINOCEROSES

A TRUE BOOK

by
**Melissa Stewart**

**Children's Press®**
A Division of Scholastic Inc.

New York  Toronto  London  Auckland  Sydney
Mexico City  New Delhi  Hong Kong
Danbury, Connecticut

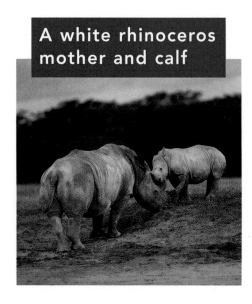
A white rhinoceros
mother and calf

Reading Consultant
**Nanci R. Vargus, Ed.D.**
*Teacher in Residence*
*University of Indianapolis*
*Indianapolis, Indiana*

Content Consultant
**Kathy Carlstead, Ph.D.**
*Honolulu Zoo*

*Dedication:*
*To Colin Campbell Stewart*

Library of Congress Cataloging-in-Publication Data

Stewart, Melissa.
    Rhinoceroses / by Melissa Stewart.
        p. cm. — (A True book)
    Includes bibliographical references and index.
    ISBN 0-516-22201-5 (lib. bdg.)      0-516-26992-5 (pbk.)
    1. Rhinoceroses—Juvenile literature. [1. Rhinoceroses.] I. Title.
II.Series.
QL737.U63 S74 2002
599.66'8—dc21                                          2001017182

SCHOLASTIC and associated designs are trademarks and/or registered
trademarks of Scholastic Inc. CHILDREN'S PRESS, TRUE BOOKS, and
A TRUE BOOK and all associated designs are trademarks and/or
registered trademarks of Grolier Publishing Company, Inc.
1 2 3 4 5 6 7 8 9 10 R 11 10 09 08 07 06 05 04 03 02

# Contents

The Horned Giant                        5

All About Rhinos                       10

Rhinos in Africa                       24

Rhinos in Asia                         32

Rhinos in Danger                       40

To Find Out More                       44

Important Words                        46

Index                                  47

Meet the Author                        48

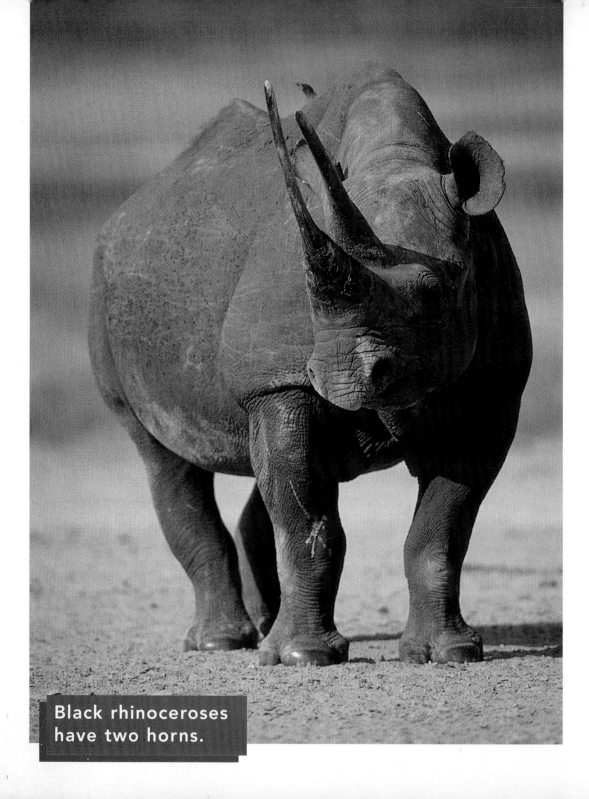

Black rhinoceroses
have two horns.

# The Horned Giant

What's the first thing you notice when you look at a rhinoceros? It's probably the horn on its nose. You aren't the only one. The name *rhinoceros* comes from two Greek words that mean "nose horned." Some kinds of rhinos have one horn, while others have two.

Indian rhinoceroses
have one horn.

A rhino's horn is made of
the same material as your
hair and fingernails. It is so
tough that it can poke a hole

through metal. Rhinos use their heavy-duty horns to jab one another and to fight lions, hyenas, and other enemies.

These rhinos are fighting with their horns.

A rhino pulling on a tree with its horn

Horns also come in handy when a rhino wants to pull down branches so that it can munch on some tasty leaves.

A rhino's horn begins to grow when the animal is about 5 weeks old—and it never stops. It grows about 3 inches (8 centimeters) longer every year. Some rhinos have horns taller than you! If a rhino's horn breaks off, it will grow back.

A rhino with a broken horn

# All About Rhinos

Rhinos have lived on Earth for about 40 million years. At one time, there were more than thirty kinds of rhinos living in Europe, Asia, Africa, and North America. Today, there are five kinds of rhinos. Three kinds live in Asia, and two kinds live in Africa.

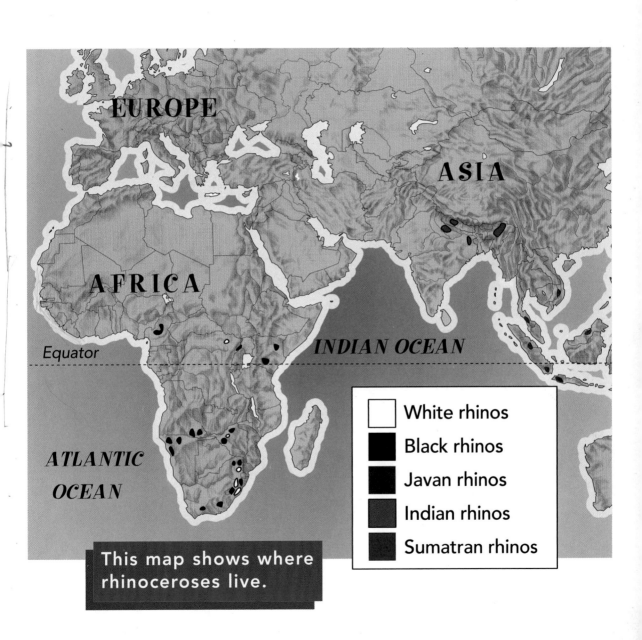

EUROPE

ASIA

AFRICA

Equator

INDIAN OCEAN

ATLANTIC
OCEAN

| | White rhinos |
| | Black rhinos |
| | Javan rhinos |
| | Indian rhinos |
| | Sumatran rhinos |

This map shows where
rhinoceroses live.

An ancient rhinoceros called Indricotherium was the heaviest land animal ever to live on Earth.

Scientists have found fossils of a 66,000-pound (30,000-kilo-gram) rhino that lived in Asia millions of years ago. It was the heaviest land animal that ever lived—heavier than any dinosaur. Today, the largest and heaviest animal on land is the elephant. Rhinos and hippos are the next-largest animals.

You might think rhinos, hippos, and elephants are closely related to one another. But rhinos have more in common with horses, zebras, and tapirs.

Rhinos belong to a group of animals that includes horses (left), tapirs (middle), and zebras (right).

Rhinos have three toes on each foot.

All these animals have an
odd number of toes on each
foot. Horses and zebras have
one toe on each foot. A tapir
has five toes on each foot. A
rhino has three toes on each

14

foot. A thick hoof protects the bottom of each toe. Some people think that a rhino's footprint looks like the ace of clubs in a deck of cards.

Doesn't the bottom of a rhino's foot look like the ace of clubs?

Though they are bulky, rhinos can run quickly over short distances.

Have you ever noticed that a horse gallops high on its toes? That is why it can run so fast. A rhino moves the same way. A huge, bulky rhino is slower than a horse, but it can gallop at a speed of 25 miles (40 kilometers) per hour for short distances.

Horses, zebras, tapirs, and rhinos have other things in common too. They all have teeth that are perfect for crushing and chewing plants. An adult rhino has between twenty-four and thirty-four teeth. It uses them to

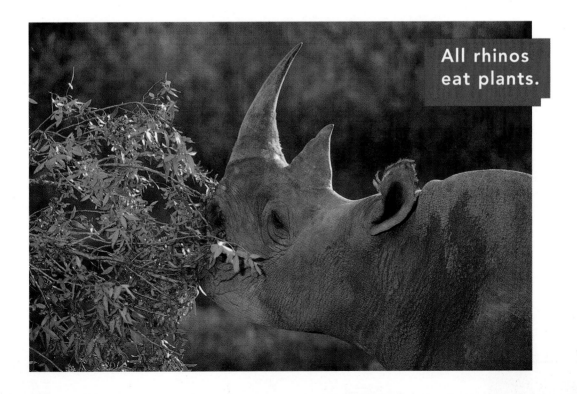

All rhinos eat plants.

grind up to 50 pounds (23 kg) of grasses, shrubs, trees, leaves, and fruit every day.

Rhinos also belong to a larger group of animals called mammals. Mice, cats, bears, and people are also mammals. All mammals have a backbone that supports their body and helps them move. They also have lungs and breathe air. They are warm-blooded animals, so their body temperature stays about the same no matter how cold or warm their environment is.

A rhino has hair on its ears (above) and on the end of its tail (right).

One more thing all mammals have in common is hair. You might think that a rhino has no hair, but it does have a little. The hair is on its ears and the tip of its tail. A rhino also has eyelashes.

Baby mammals grow inside their mother until they are ready to be born. When it is time to give birth, a female rhino leaves the group and finds a safe, quiet place. She usually has one baby at a time. A newborn rhino may weigh twenty times more than you did when you were born. In just a few hours, the calf can walk.

When mother and baby return to the group, they keep

track of each other by mewing quietly. Soon the calf starts to play with other young rhinos. Meanwhile, the females keep an eye out for predators that could attack the calves.

Like all baby mammals, a young rhino drinks mother's milk. Every day, it drinks enough milk to fill twenty glasses. After a few weeks, it starts to eats some solid food. But it continues to drink some milk for up to 2 years.

When a young rhino is about 3 years old, it leaves its mother. A young rhino takes about 5 years to become an adult. Even after it is full grown, a rhino usually waits several more years before it mates and has young of its own. Unless it is injured or killed by hunters, a rhino lives about 30 to 40 years.

# Rhinos in Africa

Two kinds of rhinos live in Africa—white rhinos and black rhinos. Don't let these names fool you, though. Both rhinos are really the same color— gray. The white rhinoceros got its name from an Afrikaans word that means "wide." When English-speaking people

White rhinos grazing in Kenya

heard the word, they thought it sounded like "white."

Why did the native people use the word "wide" to describe this rhino? They were thinking of its mouth. They knew that the easiest way to

The white rhino has a wide, square-shaped mouth (left). The black rhino has a pointed upper lip (right).

tell the difference between a white rhino and a black rhino is by looking at the animal's mouth.

The white rhino has a wide, square-shaped mouth with broad lips. This kind of mouth is perfect for eating short grasses—the main source of food on the African plains where white rhinos live. The black rhino lives in dense rain forests and dry scrubland. Its pointed upper lip is perfect for grabbing twigs and leaves.

The two kinds of African rhinos also differ in size. White rhinos are larger. Adult male

White rhinos (top) are larger than black rhinos (bottom).

white rhinos may be up to 6 feet (1.8 meters) tall at the shoulder and weigh as much as 7,900 pounds (3,600 kilo-grams). Adult male black rhinos are about 5 feet (1.5 m) tall at the shoulder and weigh up to 3,100 pounds (1,400 kg). Females are slightly smaller than males.

White rhinos have two horns and usually live in small herds.

White rhinos live in small groups of up to ten animals.

A black rhino sleeping

They rest for most of the day, and graze in the late afternoon and at night. Black rhinos also have two horns, but they usually live alone. They feed all day long, and rest at night. Rhinos can sleep standing up or lying down.

# Seeing, Hearing, and Smelling

All rhinos have small eyes and cannot see well, but they have good hearing. They can swivel their ears to pinpoint where a sound is coming from. They also have an excellent sense of smell. They can smell an enemy that is farther away than the length of eight football fields.

A black rhino swiveling its ears

When a male rhino wants to mark off the edge of its territory, it sprays urine and spreads dung with its back feet. Who wouldn't smell that! Females spray urine when they are ready to mate. They also make soft whistling noises.

A male black rhino marking its territory

# Rhinos in Asia

Three kinds of rhinos live in Asia—
Javan rhinos, Indian rhinos, and
Sumatran rhinos. These rhinos are
named after the places they live.
African rhinos have no front teeth,
but Asian rhinos do. They use
their sharp, tusk-like front teeth to
slash enemies and other rhinos
that wander into their territory.

A Javan rhino

The Javan rhino looks like it is wearing a suit of armor. The edge of each "armor plate" appears to be marked by a loose fold of skin. This one-horned rhino is extremely rare—only about sixty to eighty survive today. They live in the dense tropical rain forests of Java and South Vietnam. An adult male is about 5.5 feet (1.7 m) tall and weighs close to 4,000 pounds (1,800 kg). A Javan rhino spends most of its time munching on young trees.

Like the Javan rhino, the Indian rhino seems to have a built-in suit of armor. It lives in Nepal and northeast India and prefers swampy areas surrounded by dense elephant grass. An adult male is usually 6 feet (1.8 m) tall at the shoulder and

Indian rhinoceroses

weighs about 4,800 pounds (2,200 kg). This rhino has only one horn, but it is very valuable. It may sell for more than $30,000 per pound ($66,000 per kilogram).

The Indian rhino usually eats grass and swamp plants. It can

An Indian rhino cooling off in a
swamp filled with water plants

fold its lip to one side, making it
easier to tear plants out of the
ground. The Indian rhino is also
a good swimmer. During the
hottest part of the day, it enjoys
cooling off in a river and eating
some water plants. Like other
rhinos, the Indian rhino usually

stays within a day's walk of water. During droughts, it may use its front teeth to dig for water.

The Sumatran rhino lives in tropical rain forests and along wooded mountain slopes in Sumatra, Borneo, and parts of Malaysia. This very rare rhino is

The Sumatran rhinoceros is sometimes called the "hairy rhinoceros."

easy to recognize. It is smaller than other rhinos, and its body is covered with a shaggy coat of stiff, reddish-brown hairs. Adult males are about 4 feet (1.2 m) tall at the shoulder and weigh about 2,200 pounds (1,000 kg).

In the evening, small groups of Sumatran rhinos feed on tree branches, leaves, and fungi. If a rhino thinks there might be some tasty fruit at the top of a tree, it just plows the tree over to find out. During the day, these two-horned rhinos usually

A Sumatran rhino feeding on plants in a rain forest in Borneo (right) and a Sumatran rhino that has just rolled in the mud (below)

rest in shallow ponds or mud holes. A thick coat of mud protects rhinos from biting insects and the hot sun.

# Rhinos in Danger

People have been killing rhinos for thousands of years. To some cultures, a rhino's horn is precious. Some people grind up rhinoceros horn and add it to medicines. Others use it to make knife handles. When European settlers arrived in Africa and Asia, they began to

Rhino horns seized from poachers in Kenya

hunt rhinos and other large animals for sport.

Today only about 12,500 rhinos are left in the wild. About 1,000 more rhinos live in zoos.

It is now illegal to hunt rhinos, but some people do it anyway. This is called poaching. Poachers kill the animal for its valuable horn and its skin. In some national parks, workers cut the horns off rhinos. This might sound cruel, but it can save the animals' lives.

Rhinos are also in danger because their natural habitats are being destroyed. People want to use the land for farms or ranches. Rhinos are an important part of our world, so we must work together to save the horned giant.

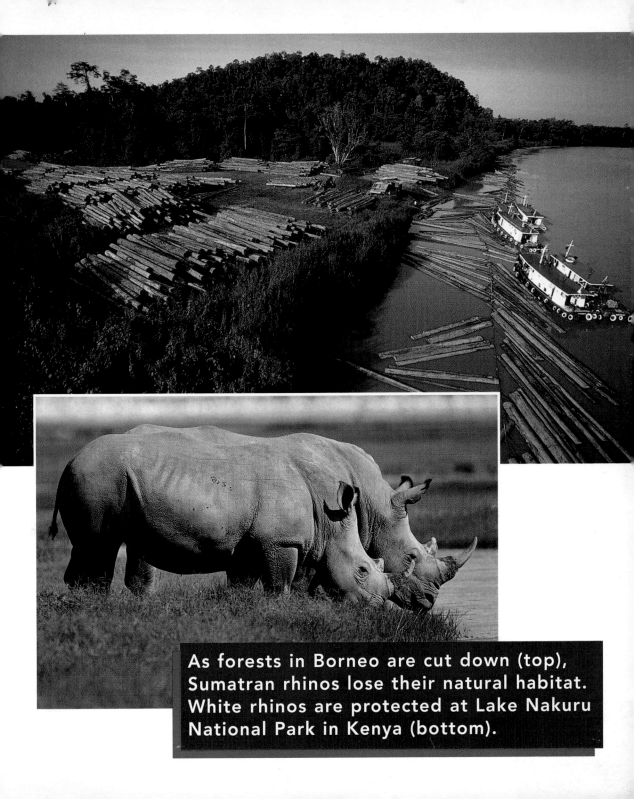

As forests in Borneo are cut down (top), Sumatran rhinos lose their natural habitat. White rhinos are protected at Lake Nakuru National Park in Kenya (bottom).

# To Find Out More

If you'd like to learn more about rhinoceroses, check out these additional resources:

 **Books**

George, Jean Craig. **Rhino Romp.** Disney, 1998.

Martin, Chryssee Perry. **Russelas: A Rhino in Search of his Horn.** Jacaranda Designs, 1995.

Patent, Dorothy Hinshaw. **Why Mammals Have Fur.** Cobble Hill Books, 1995.

Stewart, Melissa. **Mammals.** Children's Press, 2001.

Theodorou, Rod. **Black Rhino.** Heinemann Library, 2000.

Walker, Sally M. **Rhinos.** Carolrhoda, 1996.

# Organizations and Online Sites

## African Wildlife Update
4739 Fox Trail Dr. NE
Olympia, Washington
98516
*http://www.africanwildlife.org/*

This site features up-to-the-minute information about the status of threatened and endangered animals that live in Africa. The black rhino is one of the group's major concerns.

## International Rhino Foundation
14000 International Road
Cumberland Ohio 43732
*http://www.rhinos-irf.org/*

This organization is working to protect rhinos. The site has descriptions and photos of all five kinds of rhinos and maps showing where they live.

## International Wildlife Coalition
70 East Falmouth Highway
East Falmouth, MA, USA
02536
*http://www.iwc.org*

The IWC works to save endangered species and preserve animal habitats and the environment.

## KidsGoWild
*http://wcs.org/sites/kidsgowild*

This is the kids' page of the Wildlife Conservation Society. It includes wildlife news, wild animal facts, and information on how kids can get involved in saving wild animals and the environment by joining Conservation Kids.

# Important Words

*calf* young of some kinds of mammals, including rhinos

*culture* group of people that shares the same beliefs, customs, and way of life

*drought* period of no rain

*dung* animal droppings

*fungi* group of plants that includes mushrooms, molds, and rusts

*gallop* kind of running in which all four feet are sometimes off the ground

*habitat* place where an animal lives

*precious* valuable, special

*predator* animal that hunts and kills other animals for food

*territory* area where an animal lives, hunts, mates, and raises young

# Index

(**Boldface** page numbers indicate illustrations.)

Africa, 10, 24
Asia, 10
black rhinoceros, **4,** 24, 26, **26, 28,** 29, 30, **30, 31**
Borneo, 37, **39, 43**
ears, 19, 31
elephant, 13
enemies, 7
Europe, 10
eyelashes, 20
eyes, 31
female rhino, 20, 21, **21,** 23, 29
fighting, 7, **7**
food, 8, 17, **17,** 18, 23, 27, 35, 36, 38
feet, 14, **14,** 15, **15**
fossils, 12
hair, 19, **19,** 38
hearing, 31
herds, 29
hippos, 13
hoof, 15
horns, **4,** 5, **6,** 7, **7,** 8, **8,** 9, **9,** 35, 38, 40, **41,** 42
horses, 13, **13,** 14, 16, 17
hunting rhinos, 41
India, 34
Indian rhinoceros, **6,** 34, 35, **35,** 36, **36**
Indricotherium, **12**

Java, 34
Javan rhinoceros, 32, 33, **33, 34**
Kenya, **41**
lips, 27, 36
Malaysia, 37
male rhinos, 27, 29, **31,** 34, 38
mammals, 18, 19, 20
map of where rhinos live, **11**
mouth, 25, 26, **26,** 27
national parks, 42
Nepal, 34
North America, 10
poaching, 41
rhino calf, 20, 21, **21,** 22, **22**
scrubland, 27
sense of smell, 31
skin, 33
South Vietnam, 34
Sumatra, 37
Sumatran rhinoceros, 32, 37, **37,** 38, **39, 43**
tail, **19,** 20
tapir, 13, **13,** 14, 17
teeth, 17, 32
territory, 31, 32
tropical rain forests, 27, 34, 37
white rhinoceros, **2,** 24, 25, **25,** 26, **26,** 27, 28, **28,** 29, **29, 43**
zebras, 13, **13,** 14, 17

# Meet the Author

A few years ago, Melissa Stewart visited the African countries of Kenya and Tanzania. While on safari, she was captivated by rhinos. She saw dozens of them hanging out in waterholes to avoid the hot, midafternoon sun.

Ms. Stewart earned a bachelor's degree in biology from Union College and a master's degree in science and environmental journalism from New York University. She has written more than twenty books for children. Ms. Stewart lives in Marlborough, Massachusetts.

Photographs © 2001: Bruce Coleman Inc./Dieter & Mary Plage: 33; Dembinsky Photo Assoc.: 19 left (Mike Barlow), 2, 6, 14, 25 (Stan Osolinski), 9 (Anup Shah), cover, 43 bottom (Mark J. Thomas), 30 (Martin Withers); Dinosaur Corporation/prehistory.com: 12 (Art by Joseph Moravec); Minden Pictures: 13 left (Mitsuaki Iwago), 4, 13 center, 21, 39 top, 43 top (Frans Lanting), 35 (Shin Yoshino); Photo Researchers, NY: 41 (Mark Boullion), 13 right (Tim Davis), 17, 26 left, 29 (Nigel J. Dennis), 22 (Lew Eatherton), 28 top (C. Clem Haagner), 19 right (Adam Jones), 16, 31 top (Renee Lynn), 28 bottom (S.R. Maglione), 26 right, 31 bottom (Mitch Reardon), 15 (Terry Whittaker), 1 (Art Wolfe); Visuals Unlimited: 8 (Gerald & Buff Corsi), 7 (Cheryl A. Ertelt), 37, 39 bottom (Ken Lucas), 36 (Joe McDonald).